YOU ARE GOING TO DO BIG THINGS.

ELEVATE
CREATIVE CAREERS
elevate.shanemadden.com

MAKE A CAREER FROM WHAT YOU LOVE DOING.

STARTING A CAREER IN
ART & DESIGN
21 PROVEN CAREERS TO CONSIDER

5

3 TIPS FOR SUCCESS

ENTERTAINMENT
GAMES
MOVIES
COMICS
PRODUCTION

PUBLISHING
COVERS
CHILDRENS
BOOKS
RETOUCHING

CORPORATE
TECHNICAL
DESIGN
PACKAGING

PRODUCT
STOCK
T-SHIRTS
PROMOTIONS

A RESOURCE FOR EVERY ARTIST

Tired of waiting around for the work to pour in? Here is everything you need to start making it happen.

HOW TO GET A JOB IN ART IN
ART & DESIGN
21 PROVEN CAREERS TO CONSIDER

3 TIPS *

TO FINDING THE RIGHT MARKET AND ACHIEVING SUCCESS

HERE IS A COLLECTION OF TIPS TO HELP YOU GET YOUR FOOT IN THE DOOR.

BE A MASTER OF ONE

I know what it's like. We all want to work on so many different projects and types of work. How can we pick just one?!? The problem is it's hard enough to make one thing work let alone more, not only that but you also confuse your customers and clients over what it is you actually do. You need to dig deep within yourself and find the one thing you want to do first. It doesn't mean that's the only thing you do. Just the first thing you will find success in. The rest is easy.

WHAT YOU LOVE MAY NOT BE WHAT YOU SHOULD TO DO

As an artist we always appreciate others' work, but what most people don't realize is that there is a big difference between what they love to do and what they love. There are tons of artists out there that I love and respect, but that doesn't mean I am meant to do that. When I was a kid I loved animation and thought it would be amazing to be an animator.... Until I started studying animation and found out almost instantly it wasn't for me. You have to be true to yourself and do what you do rather than try to do what someone else does because you think that's what you need.

THE FRONT DOOR ISN'T THE ONLY (OR ALWAYS THE BEST) WAY IN

Sometimes breaking in can feel like storming the gates. You are just one of a thousand people slamming into a wall hoping to make it across. In this section you will find tips and tricks to break into the industry that can help you separate yourself from the noise and get your foot in the door.

The first step in any journey is always the hardest, yet it's the most important

Getting started with this guide

The hardest part of any journey is taking the first step. The hardest part of taking that step, is not knowing in which direction to go. I have found with artists and creative people this is especially true.

There are so many different venues for creating art that it can be completely overwhelming.

That's where this guide comes in. It's sole purpose is to give you the information you need to make an informed decision so you can move forward with your art career.

My aim is to give a broad spectrum of venues that you can apply your artistic abilities to and also give you an accurate idea of what you can make and if it will fit your life style or where you want to end up.

In my experience mentoring many young artists I realized that many of them had such a narrow idea of what opportunities existed. Some not even realizing the amount of artwork that effects our lives everyday.

Personally, my formal education is in technical/scientific illustration. Most people don't know what that is. Hell, I didn't even know what it was until my first year of college!

Technical illustration is the art of communicating complex things through simple illustrations, much like the instructional material that comes with all of the consumer products we use. If you take notice of the art that touches your life everyday you will see the multitude of opportunities in front of you.

This guide will give you all the info you need to make a smart informed choice, so you can break down the barriers and achieve success.

Going forward, you have two options.

1. Find a market you like and fit your work to it

or

2. find a market that fits the work you are already doing

HOW THIS GUIDE WORKS

Samples of work

These are just a few examples to give you a flavor of the type of work these markets use

Brief description

Here you will learn a little bit about each market, including resources on where to see samples and get more information as well as whether the market leans towards studio vs freelance work.

Salary expectations

Get an idea of whether your expectations meet reality

CONCEPT ART

The side door.

Everybody knows the big players the big AAA game studios, movie studios such as Marvel, Disney etc. and its ok to dream big and want to work with those companies. The reality is, there are many ways to get your foot in the door of this industry.

One area to look at is mobile and Facebook games. These studios still need high quality artwork and honestly there is a higher number of these jobs around. There are tons of start up tech companies probably some in your local area which is a great way to add real professional work and experience to your portfolio.

Also, getting your foot in the door through another position could be a great asset. Maybe starting of as a texture artist and just being around the other departments can give you a leg up on both the knowledge and experience you need to transition.

INSIDER'S QUICK TAKE

"If you're not into generating 20+ images a week, you should probably look elsewhere..."

What is it?

Concept art is a form of illustration used to rapidly generate an idea for use in films, video games, animation, comic books or other media before it is put into the final product.

Concept art is created through constant refinement, generating a large quantity of art for a given visual problem. Concept art is not only used to develop the work, but also to show the projects progress to directors, clients and generate interest from investors. Once the work on a property is complete, advertising materials using the concept art style, typically are made specifically for marketing the property based on final work. This can cause confusion to many artists not in the know who view this work.

A concept artist is an individual who generates a visual design for an item, character, or area that does not yet exist. This includes, but is not limited to, film, animation, and more recently video game production. A concept artist may be required for nothing more than preliminary artwork, or may be part of a creative team until a project reaches fruition. While it is necessary to have the skills of a fine artist, a concept artist must also be able to work to strict deadlines.

Styles

Most concept artists have fully embraced digital media because of necessity and speed. A lot of concept work has tight deadlines where an artist must produce really polished pieces in a short amount of time.

Concept art ranges from stylized to hyper realistic. Concept artists will usually be expected to adapt to the style of the studio they are hired for.

Specializations

Character Design, Creature Design, Environment Design, Prop Design

Freelance positions tend to favor a specialization where as studio positions sometimes require artists to know all specializations

The details

STUDIO / FREELANCE / **BOTH**

Average yearly salary	$ 35k-80k+
Average invoice item	$ 1500-3000

Resources you should check out

Artstation.com

ConceptArt.org

The big players

Film: Lucasfilm, Pixar, Weta

Games: EA, Activision, Blizzard, Square

The smaller guys

Advertising Companies

Design Companies (Web, Print, Architecture)

Engineering Firms

Manufacturing Companies

Boutique Game and Film Visual Effects Studios

CONCEPT ART
the art of
creating worlds

More than one way in

Sometimes breaking in can feel like storming the gates. You are just one of a thousand people slamming into a wall hoping to make it across. In this section you will find tips and tricks to break into the industry that can help you separate yourself from the noise and get your foot in the door.

Art market

Getting to know your options. These markets are usually broad titles with many different sub markets for you to explore.

A guide for being ready.

This section is meant to give you an overview of a few specific job types as well as give you a bit more information on each to make an informed decision on where YOU fit in.

The entertainment industry is one of the largest employers of artists out there. Just look at the credits of the latest Pixar movie. Read the long list after you complete your favorite video game. Take a look at the stacked shelves of you local comic/hobby shop.

There are literally thousands of artist creating amazing work in both studios and freelancing. Most, if not all jobs in this industry emphasize story through images over flash. You have to be able to create art that is not only beautiful to look at but also is able to be evocative and engage the viewer quickly.

This industry holds probably the most well known jobs in the art industry but also has some of the more niche and hidden markets. If you dig deep enough you can find all manner of creative endeavors.

Have an itch to create models? You can scratch that. Costumes? Totally. Almost anything you can think of exists. You really just need to dig deep enough and you'll find the perfect match with the skills you have.

ART & DESIGN FOR THE ENTERTAINMENT INDUSTRY

CONCEPT ART

The side door.

Everybody knows the big players. the big AAA game studios, movie studios such as Marvel, Disney, etc. and it's ok to dream big and want to work with those companies. The reality is, there are many ways to get your foot in the door of this industry.

One area to look at is mobile and Facebook games. These studios still need high quality artwork and honestly there is a higher number of these jobs around. There are tons of start up tech companies, probably some in your local area, which is a great way to add real professional work and experience to your portfolio.

Also, getting you foot in the door through another position could be a great asset. Maybe starting of as a texture artist and just being around the other departments can give you a leg up on both the knowledge and experience you need to transition.

INSIDER'S QUICK TAKE

"If you're not into generating 20+ images a week, you should probably look elsewhere..."

What is it?

Concept art is a form of illustration used to rapidly generate an idea for use in films, video games, animation, comic books or other media before it is put into the final product.

Concept art is created through constant refinement, generating a large quantity of art for a given visual problem. Concept art is not only used to develop the work, but also to show the project's progress to directors, clients and generate interest from investors. Once the work on a property is complete, advertising materials, using the 'concept art' style, typically are made specifically for marketing the property based on final work. This can cause confusion to many artists not in the know who view this work.

A concept artist is an individual who generates a visual design for an item, character, or area that does not yet exist. This includes, but is not limited to, film, animation, and more recently video game production. A concept artist may be required for nothing more than preliminary artwork, or may be part of a creative team until a project reaches fruition. While it is necessary to have the skills of a fine artist, a concept artist must also be able to work to strict deadlines

Styles

Most concept artists have fully embraced digital media because of necessity and speed. A lot of concept work has tight deadlines where an artist must produce really polished pieces in a short amount of time.

Concept art ranges from stylized to hyper realistic. Concept artists will usually be expected to adapt to the style of the studio they are hired for.

Specializations

Character Design, Creature Design, Environment Design, Prop Design

Freelance positions tend to favor a specialization where as studio positions sometimes require artists to know all specializations.

The details

STUDIO / FREELANCE / **BOTH**

Average yearly salary	$ 35k-80k+
Average invoice item	$ 1500-3000

Resources you should check out

Artstation.com

ConceptArt.org

The big players

Film: Lucasfilm, Pixar, Weta

Games: EA, Activision | Blizzard, Square

The smaller guys

Advertising Companies

Design Companies (Web, Print, Architecture)

Engineering Firms

Manufacturing Companies

Boutique Game and Film / Visual Effects Studios

CONCEPT ART
the art of
creating worlds

PRODUCTION ARTIST

The Side Door

Production art can be a great gateway job in its own right. They usually offer a lot of junior positions for which to throw your name in for. These jobs usually are not actively looking for new talent, so if this is something that speaks to you, you need to get yourself out there and not wait for them to come to you.

Another good way to get your foot in the door is to get yourself in a position to be around the creation of the work. A great example would be to work in something like toys, or some other area on the periphery of the industry you want. Then when something opens up you are first person in line to walk through the door.

INSIDER'S QUICK TAKE

"The number of production artists vs concept artist studios can be 10:1... "

What is it?

Production art is often confused with concept art as often times, it has a very similar look and feel. While concept art is often created in order to secure funding to make a product go ahead, Production art is used to take the project from idea to completion. No less creative in its creation, this art is used to bridge the gap from something intangible to something that feels alive. Building sets and 3D models can be hugely expensive, but paper (or pixels, nowadays) are cheap.

A production artist works closely with an art director, creative lead or designer to execute a design.

A lot of people new to this market have a hard time differentiating between production and concept. Although there are exceptions, things like storyboards, character turnarounds and environmental art are usually used for production purposes, not general concepting.

Styles

Most production artists have switched to digital media because of necessity and speed. Artists creating production work usually are granted a bit more time than at the concept art stage in order to make sure every detail is figured out, but speed is still a huge factor.

Much like concept art, production art and ranges from stylized to photorealistic. Production artists will usually have to adapt to the style of the studio they are hired for.

Specializations

Characters, Environments, Vehicles, Props, Visualization

The details

STUDIO / FREELANCE / BOTH

Average yearly salary $ 35k-80k+

Average invoice item $ 500-3500

Resources you should check out

Artstation.com

The big players

Film: Lucasfilm, Pixar, Weta

Games: EA, Activision | Blizzard, Square

The smaller guys

Advertising Companies

Design Companies (Web, Print, Architecture)

Engineering Firms

Manufacturing Companies

Boutique Game and Film/Visual Effects Studios

PRODUCTION ARTIST
the art of turning
ideas into reality.

COMIC ARTIST

The Side Door

The best way to break into comics is definitely to create your own. Not only does it show you have passion for the industry but the only real way to tell if you have the ability to tell a story visually is for you to actually do it.

We live in an amazing time where technology has equalized the playing field for both creators and giant publishers. Creating your own comic can be done on the cheap. You don't even need to print it! Creating you own property also lets you market it, sell it and build your own audience on your own terms.

This is one of the few art markets where "fanart" is not only accepted but also encouraged.

Take your favorite character create a 4 page story that shows action, emotion and conversation and you've got yourself a great starting point to the perfect portfolio.

INSIDER'S QUICK TAKE

"Story is king. A lot of artist confuse Pin up art with comic art. Comic art isn't a just style, it's all about telling stories."

What is it?

Comic artist is a term used to describe a number of disciplines to create stories through sequential art. These artists are almost always freelance and there is a large portion of work being created on a "work of hire" basis.

A lot of comic artist have to find other means to supplement their income due to rates for creation not reflecting the quality of work that needs to be created. Most need to negotiate their contracts to use their created work for other means of income generation.

Some also utilize the audiences they have acquired from working with larger companies in order to sustain themselves through selling their own products or services to their audience.

Styles

Comics is an one of the few art markets where styles are usually broken out into separate job titles. These include :

Pencillers - These artist take the script from the writer or editor and draw the required artwork. They tend to have the most creative input on the look and rhythm of panels

Inkers - These artist usually take the pencils and apply ink (traditionally or digitally) to help bring clarity and impact to the image as well as make it ready for mass printing.

Colorists - These artist usually take the inks and apply color (traditionally or digitally) to add atmosphere, emotion and enhance the image and story visually.

Specializations

Super Hero, Graphic Novel, Web Comics

The details

STUDIO / **FREELANCE** / BOTH

Average yearly salary $ 35k-70k+

Average invoice item $ 80-500

Resources you should check out

Bluelinepro.com

GutterZombie.com

ComicBookGraphicDesign.com

The big players

DC, Marvel, Image, Darkhorse

The smaller guys

Self Publishing, Design Companies (Web, Print, Architecture)

Engineering Firms

Manufacturing Companies

Boutique Game and Film/Visual Effects Studios

COMIC ARTIST
the art of sequential
storytelling.

BOARD/CARD GAME ART

The Side Door

There are a huge number of small publishing companies putting out small run, high quality games. They often don't have large budgets, usually only offering about $100 per illustration and some not even that. What you can do is negotiate the ability to use the work created to sell for yourself as play mats and posters, etc., offsetting the large investment in creation.

Another route often seen is to either design your own or team up with a designer looking to get their game published. There may be no budget to start but you can utilize resources such as Kickstarter to get your project published as well as building up your position within the industry.

INSIDER'S QUICK TAKE

"At a glance, this market seems to be dominated with Sci-Fi and Fantasy art, but when you dig deeper, the variety is endless..."

What is it?

The board and card game market has seen a giant boon recently. Brought on in part due to crowd funding, a large number of games are being created without the need of large publishers.

Board/card game artists specialize in generating the art and designs for these games. This includes everything from covers, instructions and designs for game pieces. Just one game can offer a huge amount of work utilizing multiple disciplines. Most games employ multiple artists in order to hit faster deadlines.

This market can also offer the opportunity to work on not only huge IPs but also smaller Indie properties.

Styles

Although a lot of game artists have switched to digital media because of necessity and speed, a ton still employ other media such as oils, watercolors and inks. A lot of game art has tight deadlines where highly polished pieces are needed in a short amount of time.

Game art ranges from stylized to photorealistic. Since multiple artists work on the same game property, you may be hired and asked to match a certain existing style.

Specializations

Cards, Dice, Boards, Box Art, Game Pieces

The details

STUDIO / **FREELANCE** / BOTH

Average yearly salary	$ 35k-50k+
Average invoice item	$ 80-3000

Resources you should check out

BoardGameGeek.com

The big players

Blizzard (Hearthstone), Wizards of the Coast Magic the Gathering and D&D), Paizo, Games Workshop

The smaller guys

Self Publishing

Wizkids

Legends of the Cryptids

BOARD/CARD GAME ART
the art of tabletop gaming.

3D ANIMATOR

The Side Door

When you think of 3D animation, the first thing you think of is an animated movie or TV show where characters are moved and manipulated to tell a story, not unlike a digital puppet show. This is a narrow vision of the market and if you're looking to find another way in you need to expand your definition.

There are some great markets out there that may not have the glitz or glamor of say working for a huge studio, but in reality you can Probably make more money.

One example of this is an architectural fly through. Ok, I know that buildings don't move and it's the camera that is actually animated, but I have personally seen these created by single artists for budgets that exceed what a major studio artist can make in a whole year. You may not have the 'fame' but you can still make a decent living.

INSIDER'S QUICK TAKE

"While seeing your creations move is hugely fulfilling, it could literally take days to get just a few seconds of animation... "

What is it?

3D animation takes models created on the computer and applies motion to them. 3D Animators generally work as part of a larger team (including modeling, texturing, rigging, lighting and rendering) to create finished video and animations used for interactive media.

People generally think of animators only working with characters and companies like Disney and Pixar, but anything can be animated and very niche specializations exist due to the extremely wide range of uses for 3D animation. 3D animators generally need to have a very high level understanding of timing and the mechanics and physics of real-world motion.

Due to the wide range of rendering styles available, 3D animation is also used in what looks like 2D animation, but is actually all generated in 3D.

Styles

3D Animators can work in a variety of styles, from realistic to cartoon.

Specializations

Character Animator, Particles and FX, Simulation, Pre-vis, Vehicles and Props

The details

STUDIO / FREELANCE **/ BOTH**

Average yearly salary $ 50k-80k+

Average invoice item $ 700-3500

Resources you should check out

3DTotal.com

Polycount.com

The big players

Film: Lucasfilm, Pixar, Weta

Games: EA, Activision | Blizzard, Square

The smaller guys

Advertising Companies

Design Companies (Web, Print, Architecture)

Engineering Firms

Manufacturing Companies

Boutique Game and Film / Visual Effects Studios

3D ANIMATOR
the art of
moving models.

TEXTURE ARTIST

The Side Door

In a way, texture artist is a great side door to all of the other job markets. Most of the time when a studio gets behind on work and it's all hands on deck they will promote from within rather than wasting time.

I have seen and heard of countless artists working as texture artists, working shoulder to shoulder with 3D and production artists, learning the ins an outs of each others work. Then, when the time comes that texture artist is in the perfect position to assume one of the other roles. Even more so because they now know how it all comes together.

If you want a great way to learn the ropes and build your portfolio of professional work, look no further than the modding community. Countless talented driven individuals have turned a fun pastime into a career and many have also created full studios out of a passion for games.

INSIDER'S QUICK TAKE

"It may not be glamorous, but texturing is crucial and can also put you in position to get ahead..."

What is it?

Texture art is a method for creating detail, surface texture, or color information on a computer-generated graphic or 3D model. Texture art is a 2d image that is wrapped around a 3d mesh in order to create realistic 3D models.

Although sometimes seen as a junior position, these jobs are crucial to the art style of the finished product. Texture artists usually work very closely with 3D modelers and may be asked to help out with modeling when the opportunity arises. Due to their skills creating 2d artwork, texture art has also been a great way for concept artists to break in.

These days with the rise of vanity "skins" and DLC, texture artist have been known to create these extra assets after their work on the original product has concluded.

Styles

Contrary to first glance, there are actually a huge number of styles to use for texturing. Whether you are going for hyper realistic or really painterly, they all require an artistic eye to be created.

Although texture creation ends up digitally, a number of skills can be employed. These include, but not limited to, photography and painting. Texture artists usually have some familiarity with 3D modelling as well as normal 2D skills.

Specializations

Texture maps, bump maps, diffuse map, UV map, normal map, light map, shader creation

The details

STUDIO / FREELANCE / **BOTH**

Average yearly salary $ 35k-60k+

Average invoice item $ 50-500

Resources you should check out

3DTotal.com

Polycount.com

Steam Workshop

The big players

Film: Lucasfilm, Pixar, Weta

Games: EA, Activision | Blizzard, Square

The smaller guys

Stock Art

3D Modelers

Modding Community

Steam Workshop

TEXTURE ARTIST
the art of touch
and feel.

A guide for being ready.

Illustrators and designers have been creating artwork for print since the advent of the printing press and even before. It is one of the oldest commercial endeavors for artists and has allowed artists to mass produce and distribute their work for over a 1000 years.

Though recent times has seen a shift from print to more digital forms of media, some job types have gone the way of the dodo while others have sprung up to meet the new challenges.

Margins have become tighter and competition has become fierce, but the empowerment of the digital age has allowed more and more artists to publish their own works without having to go through the normal gate keepers.

So while budgets may seem to be drying up with the bigger companies that were yesterday's norm, the power is now with the artist to be able to create their own works and build their own audiences.

Employing a huge number of artists with a very wide range of styles, the publishing industry is a great playground for any artist. If the idea of going to a store and seeing your work on a shelf tickles your fancy, you may be built to play within these walls.

ART & DESIGN FOR PUBLISHING AND PRINT

COVER ARTIST

The Side Door

Most big publishers have submission guidelines for which you must apply and many more require that you have an art agent or representative. I have found personally, that it can be far easier to start working with publishers as a photo retoucher or designer to start building a body of work and some credits. Working directly with a self published author, even on a series of E-books, can also give you some much needed professional portfolio pieces as well as some book credits.

When building relationships with 'influencers' you should contact the creative directors as well as book designers, even directly to authors. If an author loves your work, it's not unheard of for them to recommend you to a publisher.

INSIDER'S QUICK TAKE

"Cover art isn't just one persons idea, it involves collaboration and many disciplines interacting in harmony..."

What is it?

Cover art is a broad term that usually includes both illustration and design used to create eye catching imagery to draw in perspective consumers to purchase a product

Cover art, these days, now competes with ALL media for people's entertainment budgets. This includes movies and music as well, which has caused a shift in cover art to look more cinematic.

A cover artist is an individual who generates a visual design for any published product. This includes, but is not limited to, books, magazines, comic books, video games, DVD, CD, videotape or albums.

Styles

Cover artists are known to employ whatever techniques are necessary to achieve the look they desire for their art, and are usually hired for a specific style. A lot of cover art has tight deadlines where a highly polished piece is needed in a short amount of time.

Covert art ranges from extremely stylized to hyper realistic. Although some cover artists create the whole piece from start to finish including type and other elements, most projects are divided into there more focused disciplines of graphic design, photography, illustration or retouching and are usually overseen by an art or creative director.

Specializations

Graphic Design, Creative, Art Direction, Photography, Retouching, Illustration

The details

STUDIO / **FREELANCE** / BOTH

Average yearly salary $ 35k-80k+

Average invoice item $ 500-3500

Resources you should check out

Reedsy.com

BookCoverArchive.com

The big players

Penguin

Scholastic

Random House

McGraw Hill

The smaller guys

Self Publishers

Indie Game Studios

COVER ARTIST
the art of commercial
promotion.

CHILDREN'S BOOK ARTIST

The Side Door

The absolute best way to break in is to create your own book from start to finish then either pitch it to a larger publisher through a literary agent, or better yet, to sell and market it yourself. Not only will you learn so much about the process making you invaluable to work with, the more you do and bigger the audience you gain, means a publisher will take you more seriously. Self publishing these days on Amazon.com is fairly easy. Companies, like Lulu. com or createspace.com, allow you to do books as print on demand as well as give you access to professional services such as an ISBN number.

INSIDER'S QUICK TAKE

"Creating kids books can seem juvenile, they need to excite both the audience and narrator. Also, kids can be the harshest critics..."

What is it?

Children's book art is a form of illustration used to entertain and educate children through the use of stories and images.

Children's art is usually developed by a single creator or as a collaboration between authors and illustrators. Concept art is not only used to develop the work, but also to show the project's progress to directors, clients and investors. Once the development of the work is complete, advertising materials often resemble concept art, although these are typically made specifically for this purpose, based on final work.

A children's book artist is an individual who generates a visual designs, usually to either tell or compliment a story. These creative works usually involve humour and speak to a younger audience.

Styles

Children's artists are known to employ whatever techniques are necessary to achieve the look they desire for there art, and are usually hired for a specific style. A lot of Children's book art have tight deadlines where a highly polished piece is needed in a short amount of time.

Specializations

Picture Books, Pop Up Books, Stories, Chapter Books, Instructional

The details

STUDIO / **FREELANCE** / BOTH

Average yearly salary $ 35k-80k+

Average invoice item $ 100-10k

Resources you should check out

Lulu.com

Createspace.com

The big players

Penguin

Scholastic

Random House

McGraw Hill

The smaller guys

Self Publish Your Own

CHILDREN'S BOOK ARTIST
the art of making
smiles.

PHOTO RETOUCHER

The Side Door

The best way to break in is to compile a portfolio of a range of manipulation styles and compile them creatively with before and after images. Then approach photographers to work with. I would recommend going to the book store one day and thumbing through the magazines looking at photographers that do the style you wish to pursue. Then contact those photographers about collaborating on projects. Most photographers enjoy shooting but hate the processing part and if you can offer to alleviate that work from them you can have great symbiotic relationship.

INSIDER'S QUICK TAKE

"Amateurs rely on flash and fancy filters, but the really successful edits are the ones that look like they came straight off the lens..."

What is it?

Photo retouching or manipulation is the art of transforming or altering an image to achieve a desired outcome. Some times referred to as "Photoshopping" due to the use of Adobe Photoshop.

Retouching can be use to skillfully enhance images, but also can be used unethically to deceive the viewer.

Retouching has permeated many different art markets, offering a lower cost solution to creating custom imagery. Although some high-end jobs require custom photo-shoots, the nature of retouching allows the use of cheaper stock images for lower budget projects.

Styles

Most retouchers have switched to digital media because of necessity and speed, but techniques such as airbrush, paint, ink and double exposure are sometimes employed. Retouching can have tight deadlines and projects can range from a single high-polished image to a whole set of images.

Photo manipulation styles can range from highly polished images that don't reveal their level or manipulation, to outright stylized images showing every aspect of the manipulations.

Specializations

Glamor, Celebrity, Products, Cover Art, Fashion, Editorial

The details

STUDIO / **FREELANCE** / BOTH

Average yearly salary	$ 40k-80k+
Average invoice item	$ 100-10k

Resources you should check out

Magazine Racks at Bookstores

The big players

Magazines

Book Publishers

Ad Agencies

Photographers

The smaller guys

Self Publish Your Own

PHOTO RETOUCHER
the art of enhancing
reality

FASHION & LIFESTYLE

The Side Door

A great way to break into this industry is to start creating things on the fringes of the fashion industry.

Creating your own designs for costumes or cosplaying can be a great way to show off your creative skills. Not only that, having the skills and talent to make your own are a huge benefit.

Other ways to break in is to look for gigs on the periphery of the fashion industry including blogs and social media. They may not pay the bills to start but can garner you some publicity and get your images out there. Some people have also found success selling their own fashion art related products through sites like Etsy.com

INSIDER'S QUICK TAKE

"There is a lot more to fashion than just pretty clothes. An understanding of the human form and how it moves is crucial..."

What is it?

Fashion illustration, sometimes called fashion sketching, is used to communicate ideas visually through the use of drawings and paintings. These quick sketches allow designers to generate a number of ideas without the costly creation of building outfits.

Fashion illustrations are used not only in the generation of ideas but also communicating ideas and concepts in the construction of the items.

Fashion illustrators not only are employed in the actual creation of designs, but also can get hired by magazines to create images as part of an editorial or article, and to help promote fashion designers.

Styles

Fashion illustration is dominated by styles utilizing quick gestural drawings with media such as watercolor, markers and ink.

Each illustrator has their own personal flare and style to their work.

Specializations

Glamor, Celebrity, Products, Cover Art, Fashion, Editorial

The details

STUDIO / **FREELANCE** / BOTH

Average yearly salary	$ 40k-80k+
Average invoice item	$ 100-10k

Resources you should check out

@dallasshaw

BildonovanLimited.com

The big players

Magazines

Book Publishers

Fashion Designers

The smaller guys

Self Creations

FASHION & LIFESTYLE
the art of looking
good

EDITORIAL ILLUSTRATION

The Side Door

Any chance you can get your name and your art out there is a good thing. Artists get hired for editorial work mainly on their style and their 'voice'. These can only be accomplished through constant creation and experimentation.

Great smaller market places to pursue would include areas like blogs and social media. Listicals and other click-bait news sites such as Buzzfeed can also get your work in front of a massive number of eyes.

Serious individuals would also check out their local newspapers or ad papers to find other opportunities to stretch their editorial muscles.

INSIDER'S QUICK TAKE

"Everything in this market is based on you 'style' and your voice, so express it loud and proud..."

What is it?

Editorial illustration is art that usually contains a commentary that relates to current events or personalities.

Editorial art is usually developed by a single creator or as a collaboration between editors and illustrators. Once an idea or spin on a certain topic is narrowed down, the illustrator usually provides a few different options for what the final art should look like. The work is then refined through collaboration to make sure it speaks with clarity and impact.

An editorial artist is an individual who generates visual designs, usually to either express their own, or another's opinion. While it is necessary to have the skills of a fine artist, an editorial artist must also be able to work to strict deadlines

Styles

Editorial illustrations can offer a huge number of different styles. Everything from collage to crayons, photo realism to cave paintings. Everything is fair game

Specializations

Political, humour, Comic strip, Cartoon, Satire, Educational

The details

STUDIO / **FREELANCE** / BOTH

Average yearly salary	$ 35k-100k+
Average invoice item	$ 1k-3500k

Resources you should check out

News Sites, Magazines and Newspapers

The big players

Magazines like Time

Newspapers

The smaller guys

Blogs

Online News Sites

EDITORIAL ILLUSTRATION
the art of
expressing an opinion.

COLORING AND ACTIVITY

The Side Door

There is really two ways that content gets created for this market. Either A) someone creates the content or idea and pitches it to a publisher or B) the Publisher has an Idea and they try to find an artist that fits it and is able to implement the idea into a finished product.

Your best bet is to create your own idea and a proposal to start trying to drum up interest. If you already see it on a store shelf the idea is probably already too old and has been done. Publishing is a long process and takes a good 6 months to get a book from Idea to printed on the shelf. What you need to do is be one step ahead and try to create what will be the next trending style.

INSIDER'S QUICK TAKE

"These may look easy to create, but they can be hugely tedious to make the experience great for the final user..."

What is it?

Coloring and activity books are a form of illustration and design used to create games puzzles and entertainment for consumers young and old.

Coloring and activity books are usually created around a concept and a theme. For example, a coloring book of cities. The artist then has to generate the imagery to suit that criteria. In the case of a connect the dot book, the artist would first generate the imagery, then convert that image into a puzzle. Once the development of the work is complete, it usually has to be checked by an editor and then be layed out by a designer to create the final book

Like all publishing work, the artist must fulfill the artwork within strict guidelines and deadlines.

Styles

Styles for activity books can vary greatly depending on the idea and implementation. Subject mater also varies greatly depending on the target audience.

Specializations

Dot to Dot, Coloring Books, Sticker books, Puzzles

The details

STUDIO / **FREELANCE** / BOTH

Average yearly salary $ 35k-60k+

Average invoice item $ 200-4000$

Resources you should check out

Book Stores

Teaching Resources

The big players

Penguin

Scholastic

Random House

McGraw Hill

The smaller guys

Self Publish Your Own

COLORING AND ACTIVITY
the art of
destroying boredom.

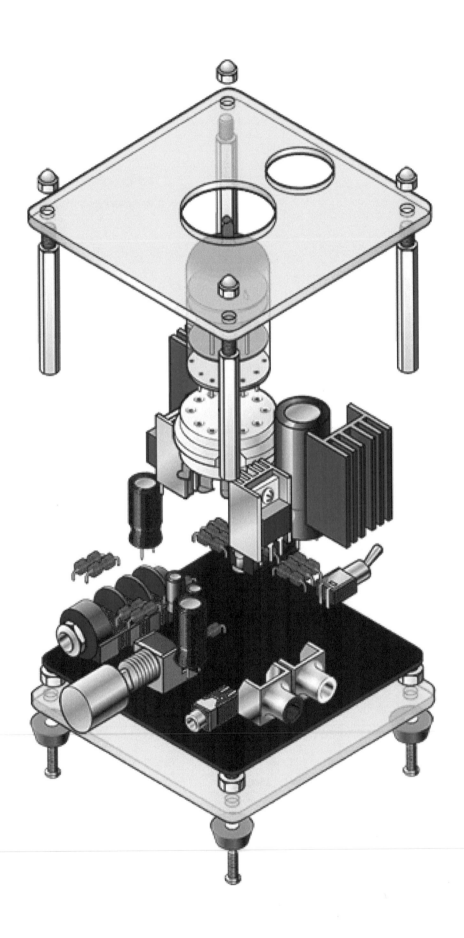

A guide for being ready.

Businesses and corporations can be a huge market for artists. Although the structure and hurdle jumping can turn off more free spirited artist, the bigger the company usually means the bigger the budget.

Many businesses view marketing and artwork in general as a black hole. There is no direct link that can be measured between creating a great piece of art and an increase in profit. For this reason, the biggest market for a creative working in the business world, hands down, is graphic design.

Large companies, even ones that have their own design departments, will hire agencies or design firms to work on projects. These groups are the absolute best to market yourself to in order to get ahead in this market.

Most corporate jobs can be accomplished from start to finish with only design and maybe photography (stock or custom), illustration work isn't always needed. This means that most illustration type jobs tend to be farmed out to free-lancers, as it can be too much overhead to keep them on staff full time.

ART & DESIGN FOR BUSINESS & CORPORATIONS

TECHNICAL ILLUSTRATOR

The Side Door

This is a strange market in that I have personally found that marketing yourself to the end user isn't usually the best choice. For instance, it's far better to market yourself to a graphic department than it is to the manufacturer itself.

A big use, and high value, for technical Illustration is for corporate literature, like annual reports. The best way to position yourself for those jobs is to market yourself to the graphic designers or advertising studios that handle those projects. Ask to have your name added to your illustration and that will lead to even more work your work gets distributed to other people in the market.

Another great avenue is to find product start-ups. They may not have big budgets but you can find a lot of interesting work to pad your portfolio with professional projects.

INSIDER'S QUICK TAKE

"If you are the kind of person who takes apart something just to 'see how it works', this may be for you..."

What is it?

Technical illustration is a form of art used to communicate complex information through simplified imagery and to educate and inform the viewer.

Technical Illustration is developed in several iterations through collaboration with many different individuals. An integral part of a technical illustrators job is to fully understand the process that they are trying to visualize.

A technical illustrator is an individual who generates a visual design for an item, character, or area that does not yet exist. A technical illustration is usually a part of a whole project and usually works as part of a team until a project reaches fruition. While it is necessary to have the skills and creativity of a fine artist, a technical illustrator must also be able to work implement structured drawing styles, such as isometric and perspective.

Styles

Most technical illustrators have switched to digital media because of necessity and speed, although many still use traditional media such as gouache, watercolor and airbrush. Technical illustration has tight deadlines where highly polished photorealistic art is needed in a short amount of time.

A big portion of modern technical illustration has been taken over by 3D modeling programs as well as direct outputting straight from engineering software such as CAD. These shortcuts have drastically cut down the number of people doing this type of work but also increased to amount that true artisans can charge.

Specializations

Medical, Scientific, Product Visualization

Although predominantly freelance, studio positions are not unheard of.

The details

STUDIO / FREELANCE / **BOTH**

Average yearly salary $ 35k-80k+ Studio

$ 50-80k+ Freelance

Average invoice item   1500-3000$

Resources you should check out

Technicalillustrators.org

Technical-Illustration.com

The big players

Corporate clients have the biggest budgets, therefore you can make the biggest margins. Because of the nature of the industry, not a lot of companies who use technical illustrations keep them on staff.

The smaller guys

Any company big or small who sells any sort of product or needs to educate their customer. You will find the most success trying to market yourself to graphic designers rather than the end user.

TECHNICAL ILLUSTRATOR
the art of complex
communication - simply

ARCHITECTURAL ILLUSTRATOR

The Side Door

A great way to enter this market and one I used to help pay tuition in art school, was to draw up free samples of perspective drawings in black and white of some homes. I would go to construction sites where they were building sub-divisions or even office buildings. I would then leave samples as well as my contact information with whoever was the person over-seeing the job, usually the person in the portable office trailer. Sure enough I ended up getting at least a few calls inquiring about more information.

Another great way would be to seek out companies who supply things to architects, such as water features, play equipment, furniture, etc., even interior designers or decorators. Having access to someone that can draw, sketch and communicate ideas fast and easily can be a major asset.

INSIDER'S QUICK TAKE

"Sometimes having a skill based on structure, like perspective, can give you stability in an unstable job market..."

What is it?

Architectural illustration is used to convey ideas and concepts, usually to gain funding for the construction of the building projects.

Architectural illustrations are usually developed from a set of blueprints or plans at the very beginnings of a project although some are created before plans are even created.

An architectural illustrator is an individual who generates a visual design for any architectural element that does not yet exist. This includes, but is not limited to animations, marketing material and 3D models.

Styles

Most architectural illustrators have switched to 3D modeling because of the necessity to show the viewer multiple views as well as immersing the viewer within the project with the use of animation and flybys. A lot of architectural work has tight deadlines where a highly polished piece is needed in a short amount of time.

Although most architectural renderings rely on the use of 3D models, some of the smaller low budget projects use black and white perspective line drawings.

Specializations

Still Renderings, Walk Through and Fly By, Virtual tours, Floor Plans, Photo Realistic, Panoramic, Renovation Renderings

The details

STUDIO / FREELANCE / **BOTH**

Average yearly salary $ 50k-120k+

Average invoice item $ 500-3000

Resources you should check out

www.normli.ca/

www.render3dquickly.com/

The big players

Architectural Firms

Architects

Theme Park Designers

Interior Design Firms

The smaller guys

Design Build Firms

Subdivision Developers

General Contractors

Interior Designers

ARCHETECTURAL ILLUSTRATOR
the art of visualizing
buildings

The Side Door

Advertising is utilized by all businesses, big and small and they usually come with budgets to suit.

A savvy individual would market themselves to the agencies that work on larger campaigns and offer your services not to take over a project but to operate as an extra set of hands when deadlines get tight. Building a track record of saving the day can win you steady and more lucrative work.

This is another market that a good background in retouching or design can get your foot in the door. Even things like 3d modelling or animation can give you a leg up on the competition.

INSIDER'S QUICK TAKE

"They may be based on consumerism, but sometimes these jobs can be hugely creative and rewarding..."

What is it?

Advertising art is a form of illustration used to entice, or sell a feeling or emotion to the viewer in order to market a product. These images can be related directly to the product itself or even just a lifestyle that is associated with it.

Advertising art is usually a collaborative effort involving many different voices and talents. Photographers, illustrators, designers and art directors all come together to show a product in the best possible light. The imagery also has to speak to many different people from all walks of life.

An advertising artist is an individual who is able to understand and communicate visually how make a connect a product to a customer. The most important skill for an advertising artist is to really get to know their audience and understand their wants and needs.

Styles

Advertising illustration can use a huge variety of styles. Both traditional and digital techniques can be used including combinations of the two.

Advertising art ranges from stylized to photo-realistic.

Specializations

Product, Lifestyle, Fashion, Electronics

The details

STUDIO / FREELANCE / **BOTH**

Average yearly salary $ 50k-80k+

Average invoice item $ 1200-3500

Resources you should check out

Magazines, TV Ads, Newspapers

The big players

Large Toys Companies (Lego, Spin Masters, Fisher Price, etc)

Large Manufacturers (Gord, GM, GE, 3M, etc)

Pharmaceutical Companies

The smaller guys

Any company that creates a product.

Any one trying to educate other people

ADVERTISING ILLUSTRATION
the art of
creating sales.

INSTRUCTIONAL ART

The Side Door

The sky is the limit with instructional material as virtually every business has some need for this. I would suggest getting a small portfolio together and contacting smaller manufacturing companies that make more unique artisan goods rather than large manufacturers. If you are looking for portfolio material, think about the tasks you do everyday, break one down and then draw out the steps.

Another great way is to find places that do any sort of product education, such as the Learning Center at Home Depot and ask if there is any opportunity to work with them to create hand out materials.

INSIDER'S QUICK TAKE

"When you stop and look we come in contact with instructional images everyday without even realizing it. Who's creating it... "

What is it?

Instructional art is a form of illustration used to instruct the viewer simply and effectively to complete a given task. Usually how to use and take care of a product with which it is associated. Instructional information that contains images only can be used by many different people regardless of language.

Instructional art is usually done in a series of images, not unlike comic art, where each image conveys a specific action or detail. Instructional materials accompany any product that is sold; everything from aircraft to small children's toys. Many products that are created have many sets of instructional materials during its life cycle. Instructions on how to create it, package it, and utilize it.

An instructional artist is an individual who is able to understand and communicate simply how to do a specific task. This includes, but is not limited to products as well as tasks that need to be repeated such as medical procedures. The most important skill for an instructional artist is to really get to know the steps involved in a process and communicate it very clearly and concisely.

Styles

Most instructional art is created in black and white line art. The user has already purchased the product so there is no real need to invest in high priced print materials.

Most instructional material utilizes projection styles, such as isometric, and is focused on clarity of information.

Specializations

Products Usage, Product Creation and Care, Services and Procedure, Education

The details

STUDIO / FREELANCE / **BOTH**

Average yearly salary	$ 35k-80k+
Average invoice item	$ 500-3000

Resources you should check out

Instruction Manuals

Book Stores

The big players

Large Toy Companies (Lego, Spin Masters, Fisher Price, etc)

Large Manufacturers (Ford, GM, GE, 3M, etc)

Pharmaceutical Companies

The smaller guys

Any company that creates a product.

Any one trying to educate other people

INSTRUCTIONAL ART
the art of clear, concise communication

3D MODELER

The Side Door

For the entertainment field there are popular forums where 3D modelers hang out like Polycount (for games) and 3DTotal (for films). Regularly posting your work on these forums and participating in the conversations is a great way to start creating friendships which lead to opportunities.

For the games market there are many "MOD" projects that you could join as a modeler. These are modifications of existing games and will give you experience with using the actual tools working 3D modelers use as well as allow you to learn how to work on a team. Similar community or passion projects also exist in the film industry.

There are many opportunities for 3D modelers locally and is a great place to start building your professional skills. As a general rule of thumb - any company that creates a product or generates any kind of images can potentially use the help of a 3D modeler.

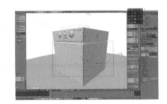

INSIDER'S QUICK TAKE

"While creating heroes and monsters can be great, don't be surprised if you spend a lot of time creating garbage cans..."

What is it?

3D modeler is a broad term for someone that takes images or ideas and turns them into three dimensional models. 3D is an essential component of many industries because it allows ideas to quickly be visualized in 3D and used in so many different ways. These models have an extremely wide range of use from films and games, toys, manufacturing, prototyping, design, animation, advertising, visualization and 3D printing. A 3D modeler generally works as part of a larger team to take their ideas and concepts and create them in 3D space.

Styles

3D modelers usually start off as generalists where they could be required to model anything at any given time, and as their career progresses they begin to specialize based on either personal interest, or due to the requirements of the work that they are attracting. Basic 3D modeling skills are also used by 2D artists to quickly create ideas and underlying imagery used in their finished works.

3D models range from photorealistic hyper-detailed models used for film, games and advertising to ultra simplistic used in children's cartoons and visualizations and everything in between. Modelers usually also have a strong sense of design, lighting, texturing and rendering which gives them full control over how their work is presented to clients.

Specializations

Characters, Environments, Vehicles, Props, Visualization

The details

STUDIO / FREELANCE / **BOTH**

Average yearly salary $ 35k-80k+

Average invoice item $ 700-3500

Resources you should check out

3DTotal.com

Polycount.com

The big players

Film: Lucasfilm, Pixar, Weta

Games: EA, Activision | Blizzard, Square

The smaller guys

Advertising Companies

Design Companies (Web, Print, Architecture)

Engineering Firms

Manufacturing Companies

Boutique Game and Film / Visual Effects Studios

3D MODELER
the art of
building ideas.

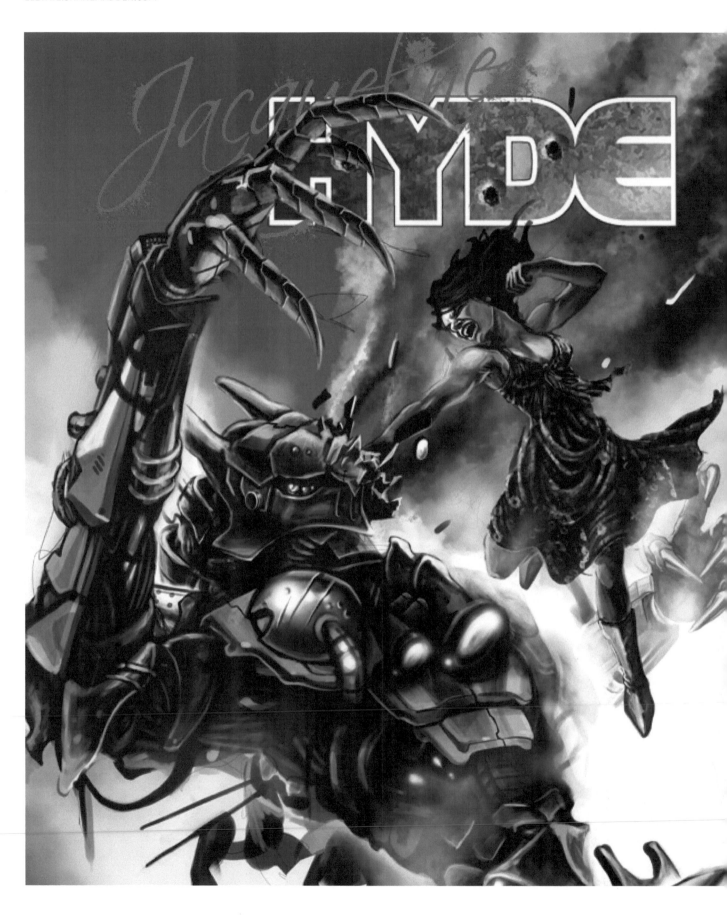

A guide for being ready.

Creating your art business around product based endeavors can be slow tedious and risky, but the payoffs can be great.

With service based offerings you are limited by the amount of time you can offer. Raising the value of that time can work for a while but soon you will find a breaking point for your clients. For instance, If you charge your customers $100/hr they may be happy, but if you raise that to $200/hr, you may hear their jaw hit the floor.

This is where products come in. You can spend the time to create one thing yet the sky is the limit on how many times you can sell that one product. Every time you sell another the value continues to go up and up. Get lucky and have your product go viral and you could literally be set for life. Having you art WORK for you while you aren't working or focusing on your passions can be an empowering thing.

That being said, there have been a large number of artist that have tried and failed. Most of which because their idea of what people want and what they actually want were far apart.

If you are going to enter the product based market you would do well to dig deep and really understand your market and customers.

ART & DESIGN FOR PROMOTION AND PRODUCTS

POSTER ARTIST

NEW M

The Side Door

The best way, and also the most popular way of breaking in is to create your own take on existing properties.

While I can't condone selling these and making money off of someone else idea, what I think is valuable is how you put your own stamp on someone else's idea, as this is what you would be doing in a professional setting.

A lot of artists sell these posters and prints and other creative goods to generate income as well. This is really illegal, so consider yourself advised.

As with all art created from other IPs, sticking to the thing that is most popular at the time could work hugely in your favor.

NINE

NINE
how many lives
do you have?

INSIDER'S QUICK TAKE

"Poster artists can spend years toiling away on creating fanart for properties they love long before they ever get paid for it"

What is it?

Poster art is the creation of advertising material usually used for the marketing and promotion of properties such as movies, concerts and video games. Poster art is usually a collaborative effort utilizing many disciplines such as typography, design, photography and illustration.

A poster artist is an individual who is able to encapsulate a given idea into a single powerful image that invokes an emotional response within the viewer. This includes, but is not limited to entertainment products. The most important skill for a poster artist is to really understand the property and the viewer and give them just enough information and excitement to make them want more.

Styles

Poster art can have a huge variety of styles, including everything from digital to silk screening. They can range from hyper realistic to super stylized.

Most poster art includes the use of both imagery as well as typography.

Specializations

Products, Entertainment including Music, Concerts and Movies

The details

STUDIO / FREELANCE / **BOTH**

Average yearly salary $ 35k-80k+

Average invoice item $ 500-3000

Resources you should check out

AllPosters.com

Art.com

The big players

Large Corporations

Agencies

Design Firms

Music Companies, Movie Studios

The smaller guys

Indie Studios

Bands

POSTER ARTIST
the art of
wall art.

STOCK ARTIST

The Side Door

Creating stock images for the sole purpose of starting your career can be a slow and painful process.

The best way to get started into this is actually to be working on other projects and positioning your contracts in such a way that you are able to also divide up the finished work and sell the parts as well.

This gives you the ability to get paid multiple times for generating the work once, but be mindful of the terms of your contracts.

The images that work best for this are things more in the corporate categories that can be utilized by other companies. If possible, during the creation process you should keep things as generic as possible.

INSIDER'S QUICK TAKE

"Although it can be very slow, selling the same work over and over again can crank the value of your time way up..."

What is it?

Stock illustration involves selling the same work to multiple clients or customers. The end user then has the rights to use and alter the art for there own personal or commercial uses.

Selling your work as stock can be a great way to turn an illustration you create to generate more income, so instead of selling it once for $100 you can sell it 500x for $10 dollars each.

One thing you need to be very aware of when utilizing artwork that was created for another client's, you must make sure you have the right to resell it to others.

It can be hit and miss on what types of work will sell well, but the best bet is more corporate looking images, including info-graphics and clean icons.

Styles

A huge variety of styles can be used to create stock illustrations, though the final art needs to be uploaded in a digital format.

Vector images are usually considered the most versatile type of artwork as it can be adapted to a number of uses.

Specializations

Vector, Corporate

The details

STUDIO / **FREELANCE** / BOTH

Average yearly salary	$ 500-20k+
Average invoice item	$ 1-100

Resources you should check out

IStockPhotos.com

GettyImages.com

DepositPhotos.com

DreamsTime.com

The big players

The Higher end stock sites will bring bigger clients with bigger budgets.

Don't be afraid to sell the same stock on multiple sites.

The smaller guys

Free Stock Sites

STOCK ARTIST
the art of selling the
same art, over and over.

T-SHIRT/ PROMO ARTIST

The Side Door

Creating your own T-shirt can be fun, but there may be a lot of trial and error to hit a design that takes off with an audience.

Designing a t-shirt for a cause can be a great way to not only get your name and creative abilities out there but you can also do some good in the world.

Using Sites like Teespring.com are great because they handle all of the transactions and only go ahead with printing once you hit a certain quota, so you can try out your ideas to your audience and let them help you with bringing it to life.

Product based creative endeavors can be hard to get started, but do offer a potential sky's the limited outcome.

INSIDER'S QUICK TAKE

"Feast or famine, your designs can either put food in your belly or leave you eating threads..."

What is it?

T-shirt artists create imagery and patterns that people should be proud enough to wear on their chests.

These days a graphic tee is a staple in everyone's closet. That being said people must really feel a connection with what they wear on their bodies. It must be an expression of themselves and is usually something they enjoy. Almost like a uniform of their tribe, whether it be music, video games of some form of humorous joke.

As with any self produced product based endeavour, the start up process can be slow and costly. Working in a t-shirt shop can give you a steady income while you sharpen your teeth and ideas while you have a steady income. These positions are probably more part-time or junior positions but can be a great place to start.

Styles

Any number of styles can be used to create designs, but adding them to the shirts themselves is usually done by silk-screening.

This technique usually requires the image to be broken into only 2-4 colors. Familiarity with this process is definitely a must.

Specializations

Pop Culture, Humor

The details

STUDIO / **FREELANCE** / BOTH

Average yearly salary $ 5k-60k+

Average invoice item $ 5-30k

Resources you should check out

Teespring.com

Society 6.com

RedBubble.com

Big Cartel.com

INPRT.com

T-SHIRT/PROMO ARTIST
the art of wearing your art on your sleeve.

GRAPHIC DESIGN

The Side Door

Graphic design itself can be seen as a side door. Many illustrators, including myself, have started off working as designers while building their client list and portfolio. The steadier nature of a design job can give you that even platform to launch yourself in another direction without having to worry about how the bills will be paid.

On the flip-side, it is also not uncommon for someone with photography or illustration skills to apply those to graphic design. There have been many times throughout my career where good work on an illustration has put me in a position to design a job as a whole, such as for a book cover, where I was allowed the opportunity to layout the type and design of the cover as well as the illustration work, which allowed me to generate more money and value from a single job.

INSIDER'S QUICK TAKE

"It's not a stretch for a graphic designer to pick up illustration work or vice versa..."

What is it?

Graphic design is a form of visual problem solving, using combinations of symbols, text and images to form creative solutions. Utilizing concepts and techniques such as typography, page layout and a keen sense of design, a designer is able to create visual compositions that not only appeal to the viewer but also solve a specific problem.

Graphic design is probably the most stable of creative jobs these days. Whether it be print or digital, every business has a need for design. Smaller companies may contract out to freelance designers where as larger companies have there own studio stocked with them.

Although some graphic designers have the skills and talent to complete most jobs from start to finish alone, many employ photographers and illustrators to generate the content that they need to fulfill their creative visions.

Styles

Design Styles change like the seasons and can vary greatly from industry to industry. Some styles can be highly structured while others can be organic and wild.

While most designers can rock a number of styles, the ones who are most sought after are the ones who have a unique style of their own.

Specializations

Corporate, Editorial, Communication, Literature, Layout, Packaging, Typography, Logos

The details

STUDIO / FREELANCE / **BOTH**

Average yearly salary $ 35k-80k+

Average invoice item $ 500-3000

Resources you should check out

GraphicRiver.net

CreativeMarket.com

Canva.com

The big players

Large Corporations

Agencies

Governments

Banks

The smaller guys

Small Businesses

Family and friends

GRAPHIC DESIGN
the art of moving shapes
and making names.

About the Author

Shane Madden is an award winning illustrator, cover artist, and technical illustrator. He has worked on more than 400 published covers for books magazines, and games, including New York Times best-seller White Hot Kiss. He loves taking on challenges and creating innovative artwork that engages people in new ways. Shane lives in Toronto, Canada, with his family.

ELEVATE
CREATIVE CAREERS
elevate.shanemadden.com

About the Elevate - Creative Careers

Elevate Creative Careers is an online resource center and education portal for established and aspiring artists who want to get more work, more clients, and more exposure. Online courses include a Freelance Boot Camp and Portfolio Revamp Course taken by hundreds of artists around the world. We also mentor aspiring artists to reach their career goals.

CPSIA information can be obtained
at www.ICGtesting.com
Printed in the USA
LVHW07n0042080918
589548LV00002B/4/P